#BringBackOurGirls:

Addressing the Growing

Threat of Boko Haram

Senate Foreign Relations Committee

Table of Contents

Testimony of Ambassador Robert P. Jackson,

Acting Assistant Secretary of State

for African Affairs,

Senate Foreign Relations Committee

Subcommittee on African Affairs

"#BringBackOurGirls: Addressing the Growing

Threat of Boko Haram"

May 15, 2014

Chairman Coons, Ranking Member Flake, and Members of the Committee, thank you for inviting me to update you about U.S. efforts to address the chilling threat that Boko Haram represents to Nigeria, one of our most important partners in sub-Saharan Africa.

It has now been one month since Boko Haram kidnapped more than two hundred girls from the town of Chibok in northeastern Nigeria. At the time of the kidnapping, these brave girls had returned to their high school in order to complete examinations that would allow them to attend university. By seeking knowledge and opportunity, they represented a challenge to Boko

Haram in the heart of its area of operations. As the world now knows, Boko Haram opposes democracy and formal education. It has attempted to crush the kind of faith in the promise of education and prosperity that families in Chibok showed.

Boko Haram, the terrorist organization that kidnapped these girls, has shown it has no regard for human life. It has been killing innocent people in Nigeria for some time, and the attack at Chibok is part of that long, terrible trend. This year alone, Boko Haram has murdered more than 1000 innocent people in vicious attacks on schools, churches, and mosques. Since 2013, it has targeted and systematically kidnapped women - including these girls – seeking to deny them the education and opportunity they deserve. The abductions in Chibok fit into this larger pattern of violence. Throughout northeastern Nigeria, innocent civilians are terrified by gunmen who come in the night to kill young men and teachers and steal away young women.

Boko Haram has also retained its ability to target Abuja, as we saw with two recent bombings at the Nyanya bus depot outside the capital. And we're concerned by the expansion of the group's operations beyond Nigeria, including in Cameroon where it has also conducted kidnappings. The group is not just a Nigerian problem; it is a regional security problem.

We join the world, the people of Nigeria, and the parents of these children in expressing our outrage at Boko Haram's shocking acts and its perverse ideology. Young people, in Nigeria and across the globe, deserve the chance to pursue their dreams without suffering the predations of violent extremists. What happened in Nigeria resonates around the world, and pleas to free the kidnapped schoolgirls have come from First Lady Michelle Obama, from Pakistani activist Malala Yousafzai, UN Special Envoy for Global Education Gordon Brown, and other champions of women's right to an education.

This tragic kidnapping demands that we redouble our efforts to defeat a Foreign Terrorist Organization that has troubled Nigeria for more than a decade. World leaders, including President Obama, have pledged their full support to the government and people of Nigeria as they seek the safe return of these brave girls. We acted swiftly to carry out the President's pledge. By Monday, May 12, the U.S. Government had deployed an 18-member interagency team to provide military and law enforcement assistance, as well as intelligence, surveillance and reconnaissance support. We have provided commercial imagery and are flying manned and unmanned ISR aircraft over Nigeria to support the search. We are working closely with international partners on the ground, including the UK and France, and we are pressing for additional multilateral action, including UN Security Council sanctions on Boko Haram. As the President has directed, we will do everything possible to support the Nigerians in their efforts to find and free these girls. But we won't stop there. We can and must continue to work closely with Nigeria to prevent Boko Haram from harming any more innocent people.

Given Nigeria's importance, Boko Haram cannot be allowed to continue its array of bloody tactics: murdering police officers, snatching children, destroying churches, burning schools, attacking mosques, driving people from their homes, and challenging the government's authority.

Mr. Chairman, A peaceful and stable Nigeria is crucially important to the future of Africa, and we cannot stay on the sidelines if it stumbles. Nigeria has the continent's largest population and biggest economy. We look to Nigeria as a partner in our quest to help Africans lead lives free of violence and filled with possibility. As an engine of growth, a fountainhead of art and industry, and a political giant, Nigeria is vital to the success of President Obama's 2012 Strategy toward Sub-Saharan Africa. As we implement that strategy, we are focusing on building a democratic, prosperous, and secure Nigeria.

Since Boko Haram came to the world's attention with a massive uprising in 2009, we have been working to help Nigeria counter this threat. We provide Nigeria with security cooperation, which goes toward professionalizing the Nigerian military, investigating bomb sites, improving border security, and carrying out responsible counterterrorism operations. As we hear reports of Boko Haram cells in neighboring countries, we have increasingly placed our response to Boko Haram in a regional context. Through our Trans-Sahara Counterterrorism Partnership, the Global Counterterrorism Forum, and our bilateral relationships with Nigeria's neighbors, we are encouraging greater information sharing and border security efforts.

At the same time, we have been urging Nigeria to reform its approach to Boko Haram. From our own difficult experiences in Afghanistan and Iraq, we know that turning the tide of an insurgency requires more than force. The state must demonstrate to its citizens that it can protect them and offer them opportunity. When soldiers destroy towns, kill civilians, and detain innocent people with impunity, mistrust takes root. When governments neglect the economic development of remote areas, confidence can falter. We share these lessons with our partners in Nigeria, urging them to ensure that security services respect human rights; officials end a culture of impunity; people see the benefits of government; and diverse voices are heard and represented in the capital. We have seen some signs of reform – we were encouraged in March of this year to see National Security Advisor Sambo Dasuki announce his "soft approach" to countering violent extremism, though Nigeria needs to follow through on implementing this strategy. We have also worked through our Counterterrorism and Conflict and Stabilization Operations Bureaus to promote narratives of non-violence in Nigeria, and we are working broadly to protect civilians, prevent atrocities, and ensure respect for human rights.

At the same time, we are providing law enforcement assistance, including by training Nigerian law enforcement officials on basic forensics, hostage negotiations, leadership, and task force development.

To counter the spread of violent extremist ideology, we support programs and initiatives – including job training and education -- that create economic alternatives for those vulnerable to being recruited by terrorist organizations.

All of this is part of a coordinated effort to help strengthen Nigeria's ability to respond responsibly and effectively to these challenges in a way that ensures civilians are protected and human rights are respected. We have also joined the international effort to isolate Boko Haram. In June 2012, the State Department designated Boko Haram's top commanders as Specially Designated Global Terrorists under section 1(b) of Executive Order 13224. In June 2013, the State Department added Abubakar Shekau, Boko Haram's official leader, to our Rewards for Justice Program and offered up to $7 million for information leading to his location. In November 2013, the State Department designated Boko Haram and Ansaru as Foreign Terrorist Organizations, under Section 219 of the Immigration and Nationality Act, as amended, and as Specially Designated Global Terrorists under section 1(b) of Executive Order 13224. Last week, our

Ambassador met President Jonathan on the margins of the World Economic Forum, and they agreed on the importance of quick action on the UN designation of Boko Haram as a terrorist group. The United Nations Security Council has renewed calls for regional cooperation to address Boko Haram. This week, Nigeria brought this question to the UN Security Council. And as I mentioned, we continue to work with Nigeria and others to press for UN Security Council sanctions on Boko Haram.

The importance of regional and multilateral coordination is clear at a time like this, as Nigeria and its partners seek to prevent Boko Haram from smuggling young women across the border or using neighboring countries as safe havens. I must note, however, that our ability to encourage regional collaboration is made more difficult, at this time, as our highly qualified nominees to be the U.S. Ambassadors to Niger and Cameroon continue to await confirmation by the full Senate.

As we strike a balance between helping empower Nigeria and counseling its government on reform, we engage regularly with Nigeria at all levels of our government. President Obama and Nigerian President Jonathan discussed security issues during their bilateral meeting on the margins of the UN General Assembly last September. Most recently, our Under Secretary for Civilian Security, Democracy, and Human Rights, Dr. Sarah Sewall, and U.S. Africa Command Commander General David Rodriguez spent May 12 and 13 in Nigeria. They met senior Nigerian security officials to discuss how to intensify efforts against Boko Haram, reform human rights practices, and pursue a comprehensive approach to Boko Haram. Under Secretary Sewall and General Rodriguez devoted considerable attention to the crisis surrounding the kidnapped women. Under Secretary Sewall called the principal of the young women's school in Chibok to express U.S. outrage and deep concern about the deplorable kidnapping.

All of these policy tools – our security cooperation, our legal and sanctions actions, and our diplomatic engagement – constitute the framework within which we are working to help Nigeria safely bring back the women kidnapped by Boko Haram. Resolving this crisis is now one of the highest priorities of the U.S. Government. As I mentioned when I began, we deployed an interagency team to advise Nigerian authorities on how to recover safely and assist these young women. Led by a senior diplomat from our Africa Bureau, the team is liaising with counterparts across Nigeria's government to offer specialized expertise on military and law enforcement best practices, hostage negotiation, intelligence gathering, strategic communications, and how to mitigate the risks of future kidnappings. At the same time, USAID has mobilized resources to provide humanitarian assistance to those affected by Boko Haram violence, including through the provision of psychosocial and medical support and treatment. We are cooperating thoroughly with the UK, France, and a host of other countries who are also dedicating significant interagency manpower, resources, and time to this effort. Our field team remains in close, coordinated contact with State Department headquarters here in Washington.

Nevertheless, Nigeria's conflict with Boko Haram will not end when these young women are bought home. Consequently, throughout this crisis, our assistance is framed by our broader and long-term policy goal of helping the Nigerians implement a comprehensive response to defeating Boko Haram that protects civilians, respects human rights, and addresses the underlying causes of the conflict. We are sharing practices and strategies with the government of Nigeria that will bolster its future efforts to defeat this deadly movement.

Nigeria's importance and the violent attacks committed by Boko Haram are both growing. We cannot ignore either trend. We welcome your interest in these urgent matters, and we look forward to continuing to work with you as we strive to bring these young women home and address the broader threat posed by Boko Haram. I would be pleased to respond to your questions.

This page left intentionally blank.

Testimony of Earl Gast

Assistant Administrator for Africa, United States Agency for International Development

Senate Foreign Relations Committee

Subcommittee on African Affairs

"#BringBackOurGirls: Addressing the Growing Threat of Boko Haram"

May 15, 2014

USAID partners around the world to end extreme poverty and promote resilient, democratic societies, while advancing our security and prosperity. Our work in Northern Nigeria highlights the nexus between security, stability and poverty reduction. We are committed to working with Nigeria to build a peaceful society that promotes inclusive economic growth and lifts its citizens out of poverty.

One month ago, Boko Haram militants kidnapped more than 250 young girls from their school in an attack so shocking it mobilized the world behind returning these girls to their families. But this latest brutality was not an isolated incident. For years, Boko Haram has terrorized the people of Northern Nigeria through bombings, kidnapping, and sexual violence.

For decades, development in the Northern part of the country has markedly lagged behind the relative progress made in the South as is evident through comparison of development indicators in Nigeria's six geopolitical zones. In the three Northern zones, per capita incomes are significantly lower than the national average. Literacy in the South-West zone is around 80 percent for girls, while in the North-East it is only 15 percent. Health statistics paint a similar picture of disparity. Immunization coverage in the North-East is only about 8 percent, while in the South-South it is closer to 36 percent.

In recent years, Boko Haram has attempted to exploit Northern Nigeria's low level of infrastructure, public services, and security. Boko Haram attacks have affected all aspects of life, from economic growth to access to basic services, and resulted in the North's growing isolation. Commercial activity in Kano, once a national economic hub, is estimated to have decreased by 50 percent in recent years, due in large part to the stream of businesses that have left Northern states like Borno and Kaduna for the stability of the South.

The conflict has caused decreases in agricultural production, price spikes, and serious concerns about food security both in the North and neighboring states, particularly import-dependent Niger. In Nigeria, nearly 4.2 million people are at risk of food insecurity, and continued unrest will likely have long-term impacts on nutrition, agriculture, and trade.

Access to health care has dramatically declined in the hardest hit conflict areas; in Borno state, doctors are fleeing and clinics are closing, forcing the population into neighboring Cameroon for basic health services.

Boko Haram has also been targeting cell phone towers so people in the region have less access to communications.

As violence began to escalate, the Government of Nigeria declared a state of emergency in Adamawa,

Borno, and Yobe states in May 2013. In early 2014, attacks carried out by Boko Haram militants killed more than 1,500 people. According to the UN, violence had displaced more than a quarter million people to neighboring states by March 2014 – 70 percent of them women and children. An additional 61,000 people, including returning migrants, have also fled to neighboring Niger, Cameroon, and Chad, where they are living in host communities.

In communities hosting internally displaced persons, the presence of additional families is straining local resources, including already-stretched water systems and basic commodities. Increasing numbers of female-headed households is forcing widows to become the sole providers for their families. Such households and widows are exposed to additional violence within host communities. In the absence of their husbands, widows also lack access to financial resources, exacerbated by inheritance laws, and systems that limit women's ownership of property.

Situational Assessment

Due to insecurity, presence of aid workers in the most affected areas is very limited and we do not yet have a comprehensive picture of the overall humanitarian situation. To determine the extent of the crisis, the UN along with key international nongovernmental organizations are currently conducting a multi-agency, multi-sector needs assessment. Last week, a team of humanitarian professionals from the UN and NGO's traveled to the areas in states of emergency (Borno, Yobe, and Adamawa) as well as three bordering states (Bauchi, Gombe, and Taraba) that have received the most internally displaced people.

This team is currently interviewing state and local officials and meeting with internally displaced persons and other community members to establish the number of displaced people, where they live, and their level of access to food, income, health care, education, water, sanitation, and hygiene. The team will also evaluate food security, nutrition, and protection services, identify humanitarian actors still on the ground, and develop the most effective approaches to deliver relief and identify opportunities to strengthen the capacity of state governments and local partners to monitor displacement, report, assess, and coordinate delivery of relief.

USAID humanitarian experts have been involved in the assessment process since the beginning, working to help define indicators and processes. USAID humanitarian experts are currently in Nigeria and will continue to support the work of the UN and other agencies. USAID will use the results of this mission to shape the provision of humanitarian assistance in partnership with implementing organizations to meet urgent humanitarian needs among affected families. Assistance may include providing food, shelter, and household items for displaced populations; safe water in communities whose resources have been overstretched because of an influx of new families; support to emergency treatment of acute malnutrition; or community-based psycho-social support and programs targeted at the prevention and treatment of sexual and gender-based violence. USAID is also exploring opportunities for collaboration with key Nigerian agencies, the Nigerian National Emergency Management Agency, local emergency response actors as well as supporting efforts to increase food security data collection and analysis to inform potential response options.

Once completed, the UN and USAID assessments will give us a better understating of the situation and how best to respond, taking into account the operational realities of programming in Northern Nigeria.

An Attack on Education

Exacerbating the humanitarian crisis, Boko Haram's assaults on youth seeking education has become ever more brazen over the past two years. A good education is a global public good, and a necessary ingredient for economic development and poverty reduction. Education enables people to live healthier and more productive lives, allowing them to fulfil their own potential, as well as to strengthen and contribute to open, inclusive and economically vibrant societies.

Boko Haram's attacks on schools had consisted of destroying empty school buildings at night, but more recently has shifted to targeting Muslim and non-Muslim students and staff with guns, knives, and explosives. The group has killed or wounded hundreds of students and teachers since June 2013. The mass abduction of female students in Chibok marked a frightening shift: While in prior attacks, Boko Haram generally instructed female students to flee, they are now publically calling on girls to abandon Western education or be taken as slaves. Boko Haram is also seeking to perpetuate child marriage as an acceptable practice and is using it to sow fear, intimidation, and coercion.

These attacks undermine Northern Nigeria's already precarious educational system by destroying schools, forcing others to close, and keeping thousands of students and teachers out of the classroom. School attendance in the region, already well below the national rate, most likely will continue to suffer.

USAID Assistance

USAID has active programs in nearly all of Nigeria's Northern states, with a particular focus on Bauchi and Sokoto. Through our education programs in the North, we have increased access to basic education services for over 15,000 orphans and vulnerable children, strengthened the capacity of 24 education-related non-governmental organizations to responsibly manage their finances, and influenced Nigeria's Educational Research and Development Council to include reading as a part of the education curriculum.

Through our economic growth programs, USAID has built the capacity of export firms, helped medium-sized, small, and micro enterprises gain access to loans, and supported the development of a new customs and excise management act to reform and modernize the Nigerian customs service. At the same time, the Feed the Future program has helped Nigerian farmers more than double their yields in maize, rice, and sorghum, and leveraged millions of dollars in credit for thousands of beneficiaries and for numerous private sector partnerships.

USAID has also helped the Sokoto and Bauchi State Houses of Assembly pass public procurement and fiscal responsibility laws, trained over 900 government officials in public procurement and financial management practices, and assisted with the passing of the federal freedom of information act and its adoption at the state levels.

USAID's conflict mitigation program—active in six states in the North, including Borno, the state most affected state by Boko Haram's violence—has funded numerous community training programs on conflict mitigation, reconstituted and trained Conflict Management and Mitigation Regional Councils, and carried out phone-in interfaith dialogues on radio and television programs.

Regionally, the Trans-Sahara Counterterrorism Partnership, which USAID implements alongside the

Departments of State and Defense, includes a regional Peace for Development program in Burkina Faso, Niger, and Chad—areas that are vulnerable as they may become fertile ground for the expansion of violent extremist groups. This initiative applies a holistic, community-led approach that has reached nearly 3.8 million people from at-risk groups through youth-led community mobilization activities, radio programming, and training in management skills, budgeting, leadership, vocational trades, and conflict resolution. In other areas of the Sahel, USAID supports a vocational education program in Mauritania and has expanded our program to counter violent extremism to key areas of Northern Mali. Given the immense size of the Sahel, interventions are limited to communities with the highest risk factors, which have been identified through assessments conducted by the project. A number of those target communities are in areas of Niger and Chad that border Nigeria. These programs have led to a noticeable rise in community action. This week, a local youth organization in Bamako, Mali, is sponsoring a mass demonstration and public outreach around the issue of the kidnapping of the Nigerian schoolgirls.

Today our thoughts are with the schoolgirls, their families; and the millions of Nigerians forced to live under the threat of Boko Haram's violence every day.

Testimony of Alice Friend

Principal Director for African Affairs, DoD

Senate Committee on Foreign Relations

Subcommittee on African Affairs

"#BringBackOurGirls: Addressing the Growing

Threat of Boko Haram"

May 15, 2014

Chairman Coons, Ranking Member Flake, Members of the subcommittee, thank you for calling us together to address the deeply disturbing recent abductions of over 270 school girls in northern Nigeria by the terrorist organization Boko Haram. People of good will across the globe have been horrified by this barbarous act and are rightly demanding that the Nigerian authorities take immediate measures to recover the girls and are asking what those of us in the international community can do to support Nigerian efforts.

Last Friday, the United States dispatched a multi-disciplinary, State Department-led team of experts to

Abuja to provide the Government of Nigeria with the specialized advice and expertise it needs to respond to these abductions. DoD has provided four subject matter experts from USAFRICOM headquarters to augment ten DoD personnel already assigned to our embassy in Abuja as part of this interagency team. In addition, two military officers with extensive experience supporting the counter-Lord's Resistance Army mission in Uganda also have been temporarily relocated to Abuja to provide advice and assistance. In total, sixteen DoD personnel with medical, intelligence, counter-terrorism and communications expertise have been assigned exclusively to the mission of advising the Nigerian security forces' efforts to recover these girls safely. Their initial efforts have been to work with Nigerian security personnel to analyze Nigerian operations, identify gaps and shortfalls, and otherwise provide requested expertise and information to the Nigerian authorities, including through the use of intelligence, surveillance, and reconnaissance support. We are also working closely with other international partners, including the

UK and France, to coordinate multilateral actions and maximize our collective assistance efforts.

Our intent is to support Nigerian-led efforts to recover the girls and help catalyze greater efforts to secure the Nigerian population from the menace of Boko Haram. The Department of Defense stands ready to do what we can to help the Nigerian government, but both the immediate and the long-term solutions to the threat Boko Haram poses to the people of Nigeria must be implemented by the government of Nigeria if a sustained security is ever to be reached.

Mr. Chairman, that threat to Nigeria from Boko Haram has grown over the past five years and mutates day-by-day, extending its reach, increasing the sophistication and lethality of its attacks, and growing its military capacity. It has now proven on multiple occasions – for example, through its successful attack on a Nigerian air base in which two of the Nigerian air force's helicopters were destroyed, as well as the coordinated, methodical and highly successful attack at Giwa barracks – that it is now capable of directly and successfully engaging Nigeria's armed forces. Its expanded reach was also convincingly and tragically demonstrated when over 70 innocent Nigerian citizens were killed in a vehicle-borne IED attack just outside the national capital of Abuja.

These most recent attacks are especially unconscionable because they were perpetrated against innocent girls and because of the sheer scale of the attack in Chibok. Unfortunately these kidnappings are only the most recent outrages in a growing portfolio of attacks perpetrated by Boko Haram in its war against education. On June 16-17, 2013, seven students and two teachers were killed when Boko Haram members attacked the Government Secondary School in Damaturu, Yobe state. This was followed on July 6, 2013 by an attack on the secondary school in Mamudo village, in which 29 students were killed, including reports that some were burned alive when their dormitory was deliberately set on fire. On September 28-29 2013, upwards of 40 students were slaughtered in a nighttime attack by Boko Haram on the Yobe State

College of Agriculture. And in yet another nighttime attack, this time at the Buni Yadi Federal Government College on February 18 of this year, at least 59 people, including boys ranging in age from 11 to 18, were killed.

The Department has been deeply concerned for some time by how much the Government of Nigeria has struggled to keep pace with Boko Haram's growing capabilities. Recognizing this threat and the need for Nigeria to adopt a whole-of-government approach to defeating it, over the past two years the United States has made a concerted effort to assist Nigeria in its counter-Boko Haram efforts. For its part, DoD has undertaken a number of initiatives. For example, we have supported the establishment of counter-IED and civil-military operations capacity within the Nigerian army in order to make C-IED an integral part of Nigeria's security doctrine. The concept is to build Nigerian institutions so that C-IED skills are organic and can be maintained and passed along by the Nigerians themselves. We have also supported the establishment of an intelligence fusion center in an effort to promote information sharing among various national security entities and, overall, to enable more effective and responsible intelligence-driven CT operations. More recently, we have begun working with Nigeria's newly-created Ranger Battalion to impart the specialized skills and disciplines needed to mount effective CT operations.

As has been demonstrated during recent Boko Haram movements and attacks, porous borders with Nigeria's northeastern and western neighbors can also facilitate these terrorists' operations in the region. For this reason, DoD and the Department of State are working closely and actively to develop a regional response to the Boko Haram threat to enhance border security along Nigeria's common borders with Chad, Niger, and Cameroon. The concept is to build border security capacity with, and promote better cooperation and communication among, the security forces of each country. In some cases, assistance would go to the military, in others the gendarmerie, and in still others immigration forces, to more effectively detect and respond to the movement of Boko Haram members back and forth between Nigeria and its neighbors. If we can build these basic but critical capacities, serious progress can be made toward halting Boko Haram's spread and reversing some of the gains it has made.

As committed as the U.S. is to supporting Nigeria in its fight against Boko Haram and in returning these girls safely to their families, we cannot ignore that Nigeria can be an extremely challenging partner to work with. In general Nigeria has failed to mount an effective campaign against Boko Haram. In the face of a new and more sophisticated threat than it has faced before, its security forces have been slow to adapt with new strategies, new doctrines and new tactics. Even more troubling, Nigeria's record of atrocities perpetrated by some of its security forces during operations against Boko Haram has been widely documented. As we have advised the Nigerians, consistent with U.S. law and policy, we review security force units who may receive assistance, and we do not provide assistance when we have credible information that they have committed gross violations of human rights. With this important consideration in mind, we have worked to engage where and how we are able to, imbuing our engagements and training efforts with human rights and law of armed conflict modules and emphasizing the importance of the broad counterinsurgency approach that we ourselves spent so much blood and treasure fulfilling.

No discussion of how to address the Boko Haram threat would be complete without addressing some of the political dynamics in Nigeria underlying the security environment. In spite of its vast oil wealth, Nigeria continues to face enormous development challenges. These factors combine with pervasive federal and state government corruption and Boko Haram's brutal terrorization of the population have made northern Nigerians susceptible to anti-government narratives and afforded the group a more permissive operating environment. The long-term solution to Boko Haram does not depend exclusively on Nigeria's military or security forces, but also requires

Nigeria's national political leaders to give serious and sustained attention to addressing the systemic problems of corruption, the lack of effective and equitable governance, and the country's uneven social and economic development.

Nevertheless, we will not lose our focus on the heartrending event that has brought us here today. The tragic situation of these girls and the families who hope for their safe return has captured the attention of the world. As I have highlighted already, DoD is committed to supporting Nigeria's efforts to locate these girls and to seeing them safely returned to their loved ones. This will not be an easy task. We are still seeking information on whether and how the girls may have been dispersed. Indeed, if this tragic episode is to end the way we all hope it will, the government of Nigeria must continue to match its public statements with a serious and focused response that draws on all elements of its government and making maximum use of the resources international partners are making available to it.

This page left intentionally blank.

Written Testimony of Lantana Adbullahi

Search for Common Ground
Submitted to the Senate Subcommittee on African Affairs
"#BringBackOurGirls: Addressing the Growing Threat of Boko Haram"
May 15, 2014

Members of the Senate, Ladies, and Gentlemen, good morning: Chairman Coons, Ranking Member Flake, members of the committee; I would like to begin by thanking you for convening this important and timely meeting and for giving me the opportunity to speak today on this crisis. I also thank the Honorable Mr. Jackson, Honorable Mr. Gast, and

Ms. Friend for their testimonies today. I thank all of you for your leadership, commitment, and efforts to help Nigerians respond to the growing crisis in our country.

My name is Lantana Abdullahi, and I work on conflict transformation and violence prevention with Search for Common Ground in Nigeria. Since 2004, we have been developing innovative media and community projects in Nigeria that encourage mutual understanding across ethnic, religious, and gender lines. I recently led a project to empower Muslim and Christian girls from northern Nigeria and promote them as peacebuilders, and I currently work with communities, women, youth, and civil society groups to prevent violence and promote peace. The testimony that follows reflects my own views, which are informed by my experiences as a mother, a Nigerian, and a peacebuilder.

I will begin by speaking briefly on the events that have brought us together today, then I will discuss some of the causes of the current crisis, and I will conclude with some practical actions that can be taken to respond to the immediate crisis and bring about long-term solutions.

The Current State of Affairs

On April 14, 2014, the Islamist militant group Boko Haram abducted more than 200 girls from a school in Chibok, a town in northeastern Nigeria. While the identity of the girls is still being confirmed, the abductees included both Muslim and Christian girls. This abduction was just one of the latest attacks for which Boko Haram has claimed responsibility. Boko Haram was created in 2002 and intensified its insurgency in 2009, with the aim of imposing its own version of Islamic law throughout Nigeria. In the past five years, the group has targeted the United Nations headquarters in Abuja, churches, the police, markets, and schools throughout northeastern Nigeria, and it has regularly engaged in bloody combat with the Nigerian military and police forces. These attacks have led to over 3,000[1] deaths, a state of emergency declaration in May 2013 in three northeastern states, and the displacement of tens of thousands of my fellow citizens. In all, Boko Haram's actions have affected more than 10 million people. It risks becoming a regional crisis and placing serious strains on Nigeria's relations with neighboring Niger, Cameroon, and Chad.

Underlying Challenges

The abduction of the Chibok school girls last month is a sad escalation of the terror the Nigerian people have witnessed since 2009. This crisis comes as a result of four long-running challenges that not only affect the northeastern parts of the country, but also have the possibility to produce widespread impact across all of Nigeria and in neighboring countries.

The first challenge is corruption and lack of confidence in the government at every level in Nigeria. Many Nigerians are frustrated, and they feel that there is a high degree of corruption in the country. Boko Haram argues that corruption is the result of democracy and western influences. They argue that democracy is a Western import that has not succeeded in Nigeria. This description resonates with frustrated, poor, and desperate people who perceive a growing gap between rich and poor and suspect that politicians are using their public offices to secure private wealth.

The second challenge is chronic poverty. This is of particular concern in northern Nigeria, which is historically disadvantaged in comparison to the more developed south. The effects of poverty on the population are pervasive: without a strong economy or income-generating activities, many parents send their children to the only schools available. An exclusively Koranic school education without other practical training offers limited opportunities for students when they graduate, as it leaves out subjects such as mathematics, science, and the liberal arts, leaving students unprepared and unable to find adequate employment. Thus, these youngsters are more susceptible to recruitment into violent groups. Additionally, Boko Haram first made in-roads with the local population by offering food and shelter, thereby taking advantage of people's vulnerability that resulted from poverty.

The third challenge stems from the geographical location of the Boko Haram insurgency. Borno, Yobe, and Adamawa states—where this violence has originated—are located along Nigeria's border with Niger, Chad, and Cameroon. Weak borders and governance in the remote region allow for the trafficking of individuals and arms across countries. Boko Haram can not only facilitate the trafficking of victims, but it can also escape prosecution and seek refuge in neighboring countries when the situation becomes too precarious for them in Nigeria.

Finally, these challenges go hand in hand with the lack of a strong civil society and media presence. In recent years, many different local and international organizations have been moving to the region but have yet to deliver a strong impact. Media programs and outlets continue to have limited reach compared to the rest of the country, and citizens have few opportunities to make their voices heard on national issues. Consequently, the local population does not trust the available news sources, leaving no suitable outlets for popular expression.

Key Opportunities and Recommendations

I have been deeply touched by the attention the tragedy of the Chibok Girls' kidnapping has garnered both in Nigeria and in the world. Their kidnapping comes after a long wave of killings, kidnappings, and abuses, and it underscores the need for new approaches to the crisis. Thus far, citizens living in the most-affected areas have seen little on-the-ground response to the crisis apart from the current offensive undertaken by security forces. Yet despite these operations, the insurgency persists, and human rights groups have presented grave reports of extremely serious abuses committed by the security actors. While securing the girls' release will be a short term gain, ensuring lasting peace in the region requires that the militancy issue be addressed from multiple angles. It also requires the engagement of all stakeholders – communities, civil society, government, and its international partners – to ensure context-specific and sustainable solutions to improve human security, peacebuilding, and the prevention of future atrocities.

While the violent actions perpetrated by Boko Haram have increased in scale, quantity, and frequency, there are a few reasons to be hopeful.

First, we have witnessed a decrease in reprisal violence within affected communities. During earlier periods of the insurgency, victims of violence appealed to their own communities, often divided along religious and ethnic lines, in order to attain justice or retribution. Recently we have seen more and more Christians and Muslims working together, supporting one another, and recognizing the need to unite to prevent violence. With the #BringBackOurGirls campaign, we have also seen a more concerted effort by Nigerians across the country to recognize the tragic consequences of the conflict in the northeast.

Secondly, in the past there has been poor coordination with the international community and neighboring countries. However, the global attention generated by the abductions of the girls and the campaign by CSOs, as well as the World Economic Forum for Africa hosted in Nigeria, have created an opportunity for foreign technical assistance from the US, UK, and France.

These two changes present an opportunity for the US government to support Nigerians as they try to respond to this crisis.

The challenges and opportunities call for a running engagement and specific actions to face longstanding problems. With this in mind, I make the recommendation for practical courses of action.

The first set is focused on addressing the human consequences of the current crisis in three key ways:

a. There is an immediate need for trauma healing and psychosocial support to victims of violence in northeast Nigeria. The psychological legacies of violence will create longterm scars, both for these girls, as well as the thousands of their fellow citizens who have lost loved ones, experienced abuses, lost their homes, and otherwise suffered as a result of the violence.

b. There is an urgent need for humanitarian support. Tens of thousands of people have fled in fear, becoming refugees in neighboring countries and fleeing to other parts of Nigeria. In some places the influx of refugees has overtaxed local water and food supplies, overcrowded schools and clinics, and competes with locals for economic opportunities. There is a need to ensure the protection of women and children fleeing the violence, to ensure they are not exposed to sexual exploitation. There is also a need to work with the displaced people to ensure that in their desperation, they do not themselves become recruited into militancy and violence.

c. Finally, there is need to begin planning for early recovery. The Nigerian government and its international partners should begin working with local communities to begin planning for how to rebuild from the devastation, including repairing infrastructure and homes that have been destroyed, creating economic livelihoods opportunities, and implementing emergency programs, such as catch-up education programs for those whose schooling has been disrupted by war.

Even while addressing its consequences, the international community can also undertake specific steps to help bring the crisis to an end in four ways:

a. Support a regional approach to prevent the Boko Haram militancy from becoming a broader crisis. There needs to be regional collaboration to work with border communities and governments to improve security along the borders between Nigeria, Niger, Cameroon, and Chad. The porous borders between these countries have facilitated human trafficking, arms and drug trade, and the movement of mercenaries. Securing the borders will limit terrorist activities and prevent the spread of militancy. The regional collaboration should not be limited to the formal security forces, but can involve local leaders, civil society, media, and governments in all four countries to recognize a shared interest in more secure and productive communities, with a particular focus on youth. Actions can include strategic livelihoods programming, community empowerment, and supporting pluralistic platforms for dialogue on diversity and tolerance through the media sector.

b. Allocate adequate funding to support a robust community-focused approach to improving human security in northeastern Nigeria. The US strategy to support northeastern Nigeria should focus on empowering women, youth, local leaders and religious groups within the conflict-affected areas of the northeast. Building cohesive, empowered, and resilient local communities will help reduce the risk of recruitment, create alternative ways for local residents to raise their concerns to government officials, and help reduce the risk of recruitment of young people. Such an approach should also include civil society capacity building and media engagement to document security conditions and monitor allegations of human rights abuses.

c. Work with civil society, religious and local leaders, Nigerian authorities, the security forces and the

National Human Rights Commission to prevent and monitor human rights abuses. This includes providing support platform building to strengthen relationships between civil society groups and the NHRC to prevent abuses in the North. Operations have been marked by reports of grave human rights abuses, and ensuring that there is a transparent process for addressing these grievances, agreed upon by all stakeholders, will prevent the allegations of abuses from becoming new grievances.

d. Consolidate the gains in peacebuilding throughout Nigeria. Alongside the crisis in the Northeast, Nigeria is facing a series of other violent conflicts in the Niger Delta, as well as in the Middle Belt. Additionally, the nation will be looking forward to elections next year. Even as we focus on resolving the crisis in the Northeast, it is critical that sufficient funds should be allocated to continue to support the consolidation of peace in the Niger Delta, interfaith peace efforts in the Middle Belt, and support the electoral process.

Conclusion

I would like to close with a personal story. Three years ago, I was in Maiduguri. As soon as I arrived, I was shocked to hear explosions all around us, serving as a painful reminder of the violence that my relatives, friends, and fellow citizens are subjected to on a regular basis.

Witnessing the routine violation of my relatives' rights and liberty particularly saddened me. Their ability to move freely was heavily restricted—even during joyous celebrations they were constantly made aware of their lack of freedom. Yet it also warmed my heart of see how resilient my family was, as well as their friends, neighbors, and communities. Despite the terror, women still went to the market. Children courageously still attended school. My fellow Nigerians were going about their lives in spite of the violence that surrounded them.

My visit to Maiduguri strengthened my commitment to work as a peacebuilder in Nigeria, to ensure that all Nigerians, both Christians and Muslims, can work together and live free of fear. I am reminded today that my experience is not unique and millions of people throughout northeastern Nigeria are affected by violence and gross violations of their individual rights and freedoms.

Thank you once again for giving this opportunity and for your interest in supporting us to overcome the challenges facing our country.

---

[1] "World Report 2013: Nigeria." Human Rights Watch.